Careers in Finance

Other titles in the *Exploring Careers* series include:

Careers in Biotechnology
Careers in Engineering
Careers in Fashion
Careers in Health Care
Careers in Information Technology
Careers in the Military
Careers in Sales and Marketing

EXPLORING
CAREERS

Careers in Finance

Joanne Mattern

ReferencePoint
Press®

For more information, contact:
ReferencePoint Press, Inc.
PO Box 27779
San Diego, CA 92198
www.ReferencePointPress.com

LIBRARY OF CONGRESS CATALOGING-IN-PUBLICATION DATA

Mattern, Joanne, 1963–
    Careers in finance / by Joanne Mattern.
        pages cm. -- (Exploring careers series)
    Includes bibliographical references and index.
    ISBN 978-1-60152-810-0 (hardback) -- ISBN 1-60152-810-8 (hardback) 1. Finance--Vocational guidance--Juvenile literature. 2. Financial services industry--Vocational guidance--Juvenile literature. I. Title.
    HG173.8.M37   2016
    332.023--dc23
                                                                                          2015007514

Contents

Finance Careers Are Right on the Money

Money is an important issue for everyone. People are always trying to earn more money, make their money go further, find new opportunities to grow their financial nest egg, or learn the best ways to make their money work for them. To help people or businesses wisely use, save, and invest their money, an industry of financial experts exists. These individuals are trained professionals who understand a range of economic fields from banking to accounting, budgets to commerce.

Because of the different skills in demand, the finance industry offers many opportunities for employment. Whether it is an accountant maintaining a company's cash flow or a bank teller cashing checks for customers, just about every business requires someone with financial expertise to help that company flourish.

Managing Money

According to the US Department of Commerce, financial services industries employed more than 5.87 million people in 2012. Every business requires someone to monitor its financial transactions and health. Businesses need accountants, bookkeepers, financial analysts, treasurers, and other financial personnel.

Individuals need financial services, too. The bewildering array of financial services and products, such as investment opportunities and the stock and bond markets, are much too complicated for the average person to make the best choices. That is why people rely on personal financial advisers and accountants to offer advice and manage their money. Even for average individuals with no investments, just doing their taxes can be a difficult task because of the intricacies of modern tax codes. People turn to accountants and other financial advisers every day in order to get advice that will help them manage their money in the best way possible.

An Analytical Career

Working in the finance industry involves a special set of skills. Finance professionals must be detail oriented and have strong analytical skills. Their jobs involve working with numbers and large amounts of money every day, so it is extremely important that finance workers be good at paying attention to details. A person who is precise and likes to make things work perfectly could be a great candidate for a financial career.

People who work in finance careers must also be good at math. They will spend their days working with numbers and poring over computer spreadsheets, so they should find satisfaction working with mathematical formulas and transactions.

A Career That Helps Others

Although it may seem that employees in the finance industry only work with numbers, the truth is very different. Numbers are a tool that finance professionals use in order to help people have better lives. Loan officers find the best ways for individuals and business owners to make their dreams come true. Personal financial advisers show people how to make their money grow and work for them so they can achieve their goals as well. Accountants make it possible for people to understand where their money is going and how to make cash flow work for them. Economic development planners can change the lives of everyone in a community by making it possible to bring in new industries and services that will hopefully make life better for everyone who lives there.

A Wide Variety of Options

The finance industry has many different career paths for all levels of education. Someone who has just finished high school can enter

Business and Financial Occupations

Occupation	Entry-Level Education	2012 Median Pay
Accountants and Auditors	Bachelor's degree	$63,550
Appraisers and Assessors of Real Estate	Bachelor's degree	$49,540
Budget Analysts	Bachelor's degree	$69,280
Cost Estimators	Bachelor's degree	$58,860
Financial Analysts	Bachelor's degree	$76,950
Financial Examiners	Bachelor's degree	$75,800
Fund-Raisers	Bachelor's degree	$50,680
Loan Officers	Bachelor's degree	$59,820
Market Research Analysts	Bachelor's degree	$60,300
Personal Financial Advisers	Bachelor's degree	$67,520
Purchasing Managers, Buyers, and Purchasing Agents	N/A	$60,550
Tax Examiners and Collectors, and Revenue Agents	Bachelor's degree	$50,440

Source: US Bureau of Labor Statistics, "Business and Financial Occupations," January 8, 2014. www.bls.gov.

the industry by working as a bank teller or an accounts clerk. Both of these positions provide on-the-job training and do not require an advanced degree.

At the other end of the spectrum, a finance professional can find many careers that make use of a bachelor's or master's degree. Many careers also offer certification and licensing programs to give candidates more education and job opportunities. Accountants, for example, can see their opportunities increase dramatically if they become certified public accountants.

The finance industry also offers many options for moving up. Someone can start as an accounts clerk and, with the right education and job experience, move up to a career as an accountant and even the controller or chief financial officer of a company. There is always room to improve and find better opportunities.

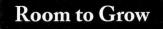

Room to Grow

The Bureau of Labor Statistics shows that most financial careers have excellent potential for growth through 2022. As financial options become more diverse and complicated, there is a greater need for professionals who can make sense of these options and help others make the most of their money. People will always need help with their finances, so a career in this field has a lot of job security and potential. For anyone with strong analytical skills who enjoys math and wants to help others, a job in finance could be a smart and satisfying career move.

Accountant

What Does an Accountant Do?

Accountants prepare and examine financial records. An accountant's job is to make sure financial records are accurate and that any payments, such as taxes or payroll, are made on time. They also make sure that individuals or businesses are managing money in an intelligent manner.

Public accountants perform many different tasks. These accountants must be familiar with tax laws and other government requirements having to do with financial matters. Public accountants work for companies, governments, and individuals. They may have their own business or work for a larger accounting firm. Many public accountants work with taxes, helping clients prepare their tax returns. Some public accountants specialize in investigating financial crimes and frauds. These accountants are called forensic accountants, and they work closely with law enforcement and lawyers when conducting their investigations.

Management accountants work for a specific company or organization. They record and

---

At a Glance:

Accountant

Minimum Educational Requirements
Bachelor's degree

Personal Qualities
Computer literate; problem solver; strong attention to detail; organized; trustworthy

Certification and Licensing
May become a certified public accountant

Working Conditions
Indoors in an office

Salary Range
From $39,930 to $111,510

Number of Jobs
As of 2012, about 1,275,400

Future Job Outlook
Growth rate of 13 percent through 2022

analyze their employer's financial information. Much of a management accountant's work includes budgeting and planning financial investments.

Almost every business has an accountant on staff or even a whole accounting department. Accountants who work for a business have many responsibilities. One of the largest responsibilities is the company payroll. They figure out how much each employee earned during a pay period and how much of those earnings need to be taken out to pay for taxes and other deductions, such as health insurance or retirement funds. Accountants make sure employees are paid correctly and on time.

Accountants also handle payments and billing. A business bills its customers for the services or products it provides. It is up to the accountant to make sure customers are billed accurately and on time. When bills are paid, the accountant must record the payment in the appropriate account in the company's general ledger.

Accountants are also responsible for paying the company's bills accurately and on time. An accountant writes all the checks to pay these bills and routes them to be signed by an authorized representative of the company.

Business accountants also keep track of a company's worth. Every item that a business owns, such as office furniture, computers, vehicles, or manufacturing equipment, has a value and is part of the company's net worth. Items lose value, or depreciate, as they get older, and in time new items may be purchased to replace them. Once again, it is the accountant's job to know the value of each item that is part of the company's net worth.

Cash flow is very important in a business. One of an accountant's most important responsibilities is to make sure that a company is earning enough money (cash coming in) to pay its bills (cash going out). An accountant may analyze a company's cash flow and make suggestions to eliminate waste and increase profits.

Not all accountants work for businesses. Some work for individuals. These accountants help people manage their money and make sure they have enough cash and other valuables to cover their bills. If a person is wealthy or has many business investments, he or she may have an accountant to manage these business affairs and make sure all payments and bills are handled correctly.

An auditor is a specific type of accountant. Auditors generally review the work of an accountant. It is the auditor's job to make sure that a company's accountants are doing an accurate job. Auditors review a company's net worth and financial transactions. An auditor is often called in to do this type of review if someone suspects fraudulent or illegal activity. In this case, the auditor would work for an outside company, not the company that is being audited, so there is no conflict of interest.

Accountants generally work in offices. Most accountants work full time and may often work more than forty hours a week during tax season or the end of a company's fiscal year, when all budget activities need to be closed out for the year. Company accountants do much of their work alone, but they also meet with other members of the business's financial team. Private-practice accountants may travel to their clients' homes or workplaces or travel out of town to conduct an audit for a company.

How Do You Become an Accountant?

Education

Accountants and auditors require at least a bachelor's degree in accounting, finance, or another business-related field. Accountants also need to know how to read and evaluate financial statements and work with accounting software programs such as Intuit QuickBooks. Some firms prefer accountants who have a master's degree in business administration (MBA).

Certification and Licensing

Certification is an excellent way to improve the chances of advancement. Many accountants choose to become a certified public accountant (CPA). In a blog post published by the American Institute of CPAs on January 31, 2014, Christopher Ekimoff, the director of the global business advisory firm FTI Consulting, states, "Those three letters really make your career." Being a CPA is required for employment by some companies as well as any accountant filing a report with the

Securities and Exchange Commission, which is a government agency that protects investors. CPAs are licensed by their state's Board of Accountancy. To become a CPA, an individual must pass a difficult four-part national exam and complete 150 semester hours of college coursework. Many employers will pay the costs of a CPA exam.

In addition to becoming a CPA, many accountants choose to get a certified management accountant (CMA) certification. This certification requires a bachelor's degree, two years of work in management accounting, and passing an exam. Auditors may also want to obtain the certified internal auditor and/or certified information systems auditor certifications.

Volunteer Work and Internships

Prospective accountants can gain practical experience through volunteer work or by finding an internship in the business field. Many colleges offer internship opportunities with public accounting firms or other financial businesses.

Skills and Personality

Accountants must have strong analytical skills. Their job is to identify problems and keep track of often-complicated financial transactions, so attention to detail and the ability to find any problems is extremely important. Accountants should also be organized; they must work with many different financial documents and may also work with a large variety of different clients.

Strong math skills are also a must. Accountants and auditors must be able to compare and interpret facts and figures and present these figures in a logical and clear way in order to keep track of financial transactions.

Good communication skills are also vital for accountants. They must be able to listen carefully and also discuss their work with their clients or colleagues. Accountants also need to present reports and explain their work at company meetings.

On the Job

Employers

Many accountants work for themselves, either independently or as the head of a small accounting firm. Many more accountants work for businesses both large and small. Accountants and auditors can also work for large accounting firms that handle many financial matters for different corporations and organizations. Because there is such a wide variety of job prospects, accountants can generally find work in many different locations, including cities, towns, and even smaller communities.

Working Conditions

Accountants can expect to work full time. During specific times of the year, such as tax season, accountants generally work overtime. Most of an accountant's work is done in an office, although auditors might travel to different locations, such as manufacturing plants or other businesses. Accountants spend long hours in front of a computer, using software and reading financial reports. They may also attend meetings and present reports to other members of the company or to their clients.

Earnings

The median annual salary for accountants was $63,550 in 2012. That year starting salaries for accountants averaged about $39,930. An experienced accountant could earn more than $111,510.

Most accountants are paid a flat salary by their employer. Accountants who run their own businesses generally charge by the hour or by the task (for example, a fixed amount to prepare an income tax return). Full-time employees can also expect to receive benefits such as paid vacation time and holidays, sick time, and health insurance.

Opportunities for Advancement

Becoming a CPA is one of the best ways accountants can advance their careers. As they gain more experience, accountants can also move up in an organization and manage other members of the accounting staff.

What Is the Future Outlook for Accountants?

The Bureau of Labor Statistics estimates that the demand for accountants will grow at an average rate of 13 percent through 2022. It estimates this will add about 166,000 new accounting jobs by 2022.

People and businesses always need help managing their money, so the demand for accountants should remain consistent and strong for the next decade. As tax laws and financial paperwork become more complicated, there will be a greater need for experts to help people handle their money efficiently and legally.

Find Out More

American Accounting Association (AAA)
5715 Bessie Dr.
Sarasota, FL 34233
phone: (941) 921-7747
website: www.aaahq.org

The AAA is the largest community of accountants in the academic world. This organization focuses on educating accounting professionals through research and teaching, and also offers the AAA Awards to reward research projects by accounting students and professionals.

American Institute of Certified Public Accountants (AICPA)
1211 Avenue of the Americas
New York, NY 10036
phone: (212) 596-6200
website: www.aicpa.org

The AICPA is the world's largest organization representing accountants. The AICPA develops and grades the Uniform CPA Examination and offers certification in specific fields such as auditing, financial planning, forensic accounting, and more. This organization also offers scholarships as well as a wealth of information on every aspect of the accounting profession.

Institute of Internal Auditors (IIA)
247 Maitland Ave.
Altamonte Springs, FL 32701
phone: (407) 937-1111
website: www.theiia.org

Established in 1941, the IIA is an international organization for members working in internal auditing, risk management, information technology auditing, internal control, and other accounting specialties. The IIA offers the certified internal auditor certification as well as several other certification exams and programs for auditors.

Institute of Management Accountants
10 Paragon Dr., Suite 1
Montvale, NJ 07645
phone: (800) 638-4427
website: www.imanet.org

This organization offers the CMA certification to applicants. It is a worldwide organization whose goal is to empower accountants and other business professionals to expand professional skills and enhance their careers.

National Society of Accountants (NSA)
1010 N. Fairfax St.
Alexandria, VA 22314
phone: (800) 966-6679
website: www.nsacct.org

The NSA provides national leadership and helps its members achieve success in the fields of accounting and taxation. It promotes high standards in education and professional ethics and supports its members with continuing education programs, professional guidance, and scholarships for students in the accounting field.

Accounts Clerk

What Does an Accounts Clerk Do?

All businesses and organizations keep financial records. They need to accurately record expenses, such as payments to creditors (people or companies to whom the organization owes money), as well as income. Companies rely on accounts clerks to keep these financial records. Accounts clerks produce financial records for companies or organizations. They record financial transactions, update statements, and check financial records for accuracy. An accounts clerk is responsible for gathering and entering data into the company's financial system. This is a lower-level job than an accountant, who is responsible for overseeing accounts and has knowledge of a wider variety of accounting practices.

Accounts clerks typically use bookkeeping software, online spreadsheets, and other computer programs to keep track of a business's income and expenses. Clerks enter, or post, financial transactions into the accounting software. Each transaction must be placed into a specific account.

An accounts clerk may also handle payments. He or she

At a Glance:
Accounts Clerk

Minimum Educational Requirements
High school diploma or equivalent

Personal Qualities
Computer literate; detail oriented and organized; trustworthy

Certification and Licensing
Certification is recommended

Working Conditions
Indoors in an office

Salary Range
From $21,610 to $54,310

Number of Jobs
As of 2012 about 1,799,800

Future Job Outlook
Growth rate of 11 percent through 2022

is responsible for receiving and recording all financial transactions, which may be made by cash, check, or credit.

Accounts clerks also produce reports to show the company's financial activities. These reports can include income statements, expense statements, or balance sheets, which compare income to costs. Accounts clerks also check for accuracy in all reports and are responsible for reporting any differences they find. In some cases, accounts clerks may also be asked to reconcile, or fix, these differences.

There are different types of accounts clerks. Bookkeeping clerks are responsible for some or all of an organization's accounts. They post all transactions by recording them into a document called the general ledger. Bookkeeping clerks may also produce financial statements and other reports. They may also prepare bank deposits by verifying receipts, preparing deposit tickets, and sending cash, checks, or other forms of payment to the bank. Some companies, especially ones with a small staff, may require bookkeeping clerks to prepare payroll, make purchases, prepare invoices, and keep track of overdue accounts.

Accounting clerks usually work for larger companies and have more specialized tasks than bookkeeping clerks. For example, whereas an accounts receivable clerk would only work with payments received by the company (income), an accounts payable clerk would focus on payments the company made to others (expenses). An accounting clerk's responsibilities can increase with experience. An entry-level clerk may post only financial transactions to the general ledger and do other simple accounting tasks. A more senior accounting clerk might balance the ledger, make sure that account data is accurate, and perform more sophisticated computer coding of financial documents.

Auditing clerks are responsible for checking and correcting work by other accounting clerks or accountants. These clerks check figures, general ledger postings, and other documents to make sure they are accurate. They may also correct errors or alert more senior staff members to a problem.

Accounts clerks work in offices and spend most of their time on computers. Most accounts clerks work full time, but others may work part time, especially if they are employed by a small business or organization. It is not unusual for accounts clerks to work more than forty hours a week during tax season or certain times during the fiscal year.

Accounts clerks often work alone, but they also can be part of a company's accounting team. They may work with accountants, clerks from other departments, or other members of a company's finance department.

How Do You Become an Accounts Clerk?

Education

Accounts clerks need a high school diploma in order to find work, although some companies prefer to hire clerks who have taken college courses in accounting or bookkeeping. Accounts clerks should have a strong background in math and computer skills and know how to use spreadsheets and bookkeeping software such as Intuit QuickBooks. It is very common for accounts clerks to learn some of their skills on the job and be trained by their employers to perform specific tasks.

Certification and Licensing

Certification is available for some accounts clerks, particularly bookkeepers. The bookkeeper certification, which is awarded by the American Institute of Professional Bookkeepers, declares that the clerk has the skills and knowledge to perform all bookkeeping tasks, including payroll. To obtain certification, candidates must have at least two years of full-time experience as a bookkeeping clerk, pass a four-part exam, and follow a strict code of ethics. The National Association of Certified Public Bookkeepers also offers a certification called the uniform bookkeeper certification. Clerks can obtain this certification by scoring 80 percent or better on an online test.

Volunteer Work and Internships

Accounts clerks can gain practical experience through volunteer work or by finding an internship in the business field. Many colleges offer internship opportunities with businesses.

Skills and Personality

Accounts clerks must be detail oriented. It is very important that clerks produce accurate financial records and pay close attention so figures are entered correctly. Because accounts clerks deal with numbers all day, they should have strong math skills as well. Similarly, since most accounting work is done on computers, accounts clerks should be comfortable using computer software.

It is essential that accounts clerks be honest and ethical. These clerks have inside knowledge of a company's financial documents and control the company's financial transactions. Accounts clerks should be extremely honest and always guard against any fraud or other illegal activity.

Employers

Accounts clerks can work for a variety of different companies, both large and small. They may also work for organizations, such as non-profit, charitable, or community groups. Whereas a large company may have many accounts clerks working for it, a small company might have just one or two clerks to handle its accounts. The wide variety of employment opportunities means that accounts clerks can find work in many different locations and businesses.

Working Conditions

Many accounts clerks work full time. This is especially true of clerks who work for large companies. Clerks may be expected to work overtime during tax season and other times of the year. The majority of an accounts clerk's work is done on a computer in an office.

Other accounts clerks work part time, especially if they work for a smaller business or organization. Some clerks may work several part-time jobs for different employers.

Earnings

The median annual salary for accounts clerks was $35,170 in 2012. That year starting salaries for accounts clerks averaged about $21,610, and the highest salaries were more than $54,310.

Depending on the employer, an accounts clerk might be paid a flat salary or an hourly wage. The Bureau of Labor Statistics reports that the median hourly wage for an accounts clerk was $16.91 in 2012.

Full-time employees can also expect to receive benefits such as paid vacation time and holidays, sick time, and health insurance. Hourly or part-time employees are not likely to receive these benefits.

Opportunities for Advancement

Some accounts clerks can advance to higher positions as accountants or auditors. To advance, clerks need to obtain both work experience and further education, and they may need to become certified for a particular field. Accounting certifications include the CPA and CMA certifications. (You can learn more about these certifications in chapter 1.)

What Is the Future Outlook for Accounts Clerks?

The Bureau of Labor Statistics estimates that the demand for accounts clerks will grow at a rate of 11 percent through 2022. This is an average rate of growth that will add an estimated 204,600 new jobs in this field by 2022. There are always businesses and organizations that need accounts clerks, including small start-up businesses. Because of this, the demand for accounts clerks should remain steady.

Find Out More

American Institute of Professional Bookkeepers (AIPB)
6001 Montrose Rd., Suite 500
Rockville, MD 20852
phone: (800) 622-0121
website: www.aipb.org

The AIPB was established in 1987 to support bookkeepers and promote this financial profession. The AIPB offers opportunities for networking, educational advancement, and job searching as well as a bookkeeping certification program.

American Payroll Association
660 N. Main Ave., Suite 100
San Antonio, TX 78205
phone: (210) 226-4600
website: www.americanpayroll.org

The American Payroll Association provides webinars and other information geared to people who work in payroll accounting. It provides certification, networking opportunities, a job board, and other resources to help its members excel in this field.

National Association of Certified Public Bookkeepers (NACPB)
283 N. 300 W., Suite 504
Kaysville, UT 84037
phone: (866) 444-9989
website: www.nacpb.org

The NACPB calls itself the "only national bookkeeping organization dedicated exclusively to the needs of bookkeeping professionals." It offers a uniform bookkeeper certification test as well as certifications in Intuit QuickBooks, payroll, taxes, and Microsoft Excel. The NACPB also offers educational and professional opportunities for bookkeeping clerks to advance their careers.

Bank Teller

Bank tellers are the public face of the banking industry. They work directly with the public to process routine transactions at banks. Bank tellers have to interact with customers all day long and help them perform their financial transactions, such as depositing money or cashing checks.

Because they handle large amounts of money, bank tellers must follow a strict routine at work. They start the day by counting the money in their drawer and recording how much cash is there. During the day they accept checks and cash payments from customers and add this money to the drawer. They also deduct money from the drawer and give it to a customer who is cashing a check or withdrawing money from an account. All transactions are also recorded electronically by posting them on a computer. At the end of the day the bank teller again counts the money in the drawer and checks to see if it matches the amount that the computer says should be there. This process is called *proving*.

Bank tellers perform many other duties besides cashing checks and accepting payments.

At a Glance:

Bank Teller

Minimum Educational Requirements
High school diploma

Personal Qualities
Excellent customer service; good at basic math; computer literate; detail oriented; trustworthy

Certification and Licensing
None required

Working Conditions
Indoors in bank branches

Salary Range
From $19,630 to $34,320

Number of Jobs
As of 2012 about 545,300

Future Job Outlook
Growth rate of 1 percent through 2022

Bank tellers work directly with the public to process routine transactions such as depositing money and cashing checks. Because they work with customers and handle large amounts of money, they must be good with people and numbers and they must be able to follow strict procedures.

They also answer questions from customers about their accounts, such as when a payment was made. They can also order new checks or debit cards for customers to use.

Tellers may also prepare special types of funds, such as traveler's checks, savings bonds, and money transfers. Some banks offer foreign currency, so a teller working at one of these banks would figure out the exchange rate to change US money into a foreign currency, then provide the customer with the correct amount of foreign cash.

When working with the public, bank tellers must be responsible and meticulous. For example, before cashing a check, the teller must verify that the customer has an account at the bank, see the customer's identification, and make sure he or she has enough money in the bank account to cover the amount of the check. Bank tellers must also be very careful when counting cash so they do not make any errors and give the customer too much or too little money.

Bank tellers may also help open new accounts for customers. They will talk to the customer about what his or her needs are, check identification, and provide the appropriate paperwork for the customer to open an account.

Banks offer many different financial products, and many banks expect their tellers to sell these products to customers. Some of these products are special accounts called certificates of deposit or money market accounts, both of which offer a higher rate of interest than regular savings accounts. Banks also offer many different types of credit cards. Bank tellers often ask customers if they are interested in obtaining a card and explain the terms of the card and what benefits it offers. Tellers also may offer a new product or service to a customer based on the information the teller has about the customer's accounts.

Some bank tellers with enough experience become head tellers. Head tellers supervise the other tellers and help them resolve problems. They may also help customers obtain services such as business loans or other bank services.

Bank tellers work in bank branches. These banks can be very large, nationally known institutions, or they can be smaller community banks or credit unions. Tellers usually work with a few other tellers as well as other bank personnel. Because they work behind a counter, they may be asked to stand all day as they wait on customers.

Many bank tellers enjoy their job because they enjoy interacting with people. Bank tellers help people with financial transactions and offer products and services that can help their customers. They often get to know their customers because they see them so often and spend time talking to them.

How Do You Become a Bank Teller?

Education

Most bank tellers have a high school diploma. They also receive on-the-job training, which lasts, on average, one month. This training includes how to balance a cash drawer, how to verify identification and signatures, how to use the bank's computer software, and what other products and services the bank offers.

Certification and Licensing

No certification or licensing is required for this occupation. However, some colleges offer bank teller certificate programs. A bank teller certificate program teaches students to interact with customers and perform basic banking duties. Students also learn various financial calculations and formulas and gain knowledge of different computer systems. Most programs require one to three semesters of study and include courses covering the principles of banking, handling cash, financial operations, electronic calculations, customer service, and business communications.

Bank tellers can also obtain voluntary certification from the American Bankers Association (ABA). The ABA offers a bank teller certification to tellers with at least six months of job experience. These tellers must also complete the American Institute of Banking's bank teller certificate program, provide professional references, and pass a rigorous exam.

Volunteer Work and Internships

Although it is unlikely that a bank teller would find volunteer work or internships in this field, candidates can prepare by volunteering or interning at businesses that handle financial transactions and include customer service responsibilities.

Skills and Personality

Bank tellers must have excellent customer service skills. They will spend their entire working day dealing with the public. This can be enjoyable because tellers get to meet many different types of people. However, some customers can be difficult and unpleasant, which can be stressful. It is important that bank tellers be polite, pleasant, and helpful even in difficult situations.

Bank tellers should also have excellent math skills and be comfortable performing financial transactions. Because they spend their workday handling money, they should be detail oriented and careful not to make mistakes. In addition, bank tellers should have integrity and be trustworthy.

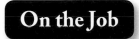

On the Job

Employers

Bank tellers work in branch locations of financial institutions. These banks can be large or small and be located in any type of environment, from big cities to rural areas. Tellers may also be employed by other financial institutions, such as credit unions.

Working Conditions

Bank tellers may work full or part time. The majority of a bank teller's day is spent on his or her feet standing behind a counter. Although most banks are open on weekdays, many now offer hours on weekends as well. A bank teller might be asked to work on weekends or on a rotating schedule to cover weekend shifts.

Earnings

The median annual salary for bank tellers was $24,940 in 2012. During that same year starting salaries for bank tellers averaged about $19,630. The top 10 percent earned more than $34,320.

Depending on the bank where he or she works, a bank teller might be paid a flat salary or an hourly wage. The Bureau of Labor Statistics reports that the median hourly wage for a bank teller was about $12 in 2012.

Full-time employees can also expect to receive benefits such as paid vacation time and holidays, sick time, and health insurance. Hourly or part-time employees are not likely to receive these benefits.

Opportunities for Advancement

Bank tellers can advance to the position of head teller. Head tellers perform managerial duties, such as setting work schedules, supervising other tellers, or training new employees. Head tellers may also be asked to resolve customer account errors or handle customer problems.

Experienced tellers often move to advanced positions within their bank or other banks. They can move to sales positions or work as loan officers. With more training and education, some tellers may choose to move into financial planning, accounting, or other finance-related fields.

What Is the Future Outlook for Bank Tellers?

The Bureau of Labor Statistics estimates that there will be little or no change in the demand for bank tellers. The bureau expects demand to grow only at a rate of 1 percent through 2022, adding only fifty-six hundred new jobs.

This slow rate of growth is mostly due to the increased automation in the banking industry. Many customers now use online banking or go to an ATM to deposit checks or withdraw money. In addition, many workers are paid by electronic funds transfers or direct deposit and no longer have the need to cash checks.

However, many bank tellers do not stay at this job for a long time. Many use it as a stepping stone to more advanced careers in the finance industry. This constant turnover means there are usually openings for new tellers at banks around the nation.

Find Out More

American Bankers Association (ABA)
1120 Connecticut Ave. NW
Washington, DC 20036
phone: (800) 226-5377
website: www.aba.com

The ABA represents American banks of all sizes. The ABA lobbies the government for fair banking laws and policies and also offers professional development, training, job networking, and other resources to banks and their employees. The ABA also offers a bank teller certificate program through its American Institute of Banking.

BAI
115 S. LaSalle St., Suite 3300
Chicago, IL 60603
phone: (888) 224-0037
website: www.bai.org

BAI calls itself "a financial services organization and leading industry resource." It offers information, education, research, and networking opportunities for members of the banking industry, from large multinational organizations to small community banks.

Independent Community Bankers of America (ICBA)
1615 L St. NW, Suite 900
Washington, DC 20036
phone: (800) 422-8439
website: www.icba.org

The ICBA represents more than sixty-five hundred community banks of all sizes across the United States. The organization is dedicated to representing their interests and providing educational courses and certification programs to help bankers better serve the people of their communities.

National Bankers Association (NBA)
1513 P St. NW
Washington, DC 20005
phone: (202) 588-5432
website: www.nationalbankers.org

The NBA is a banking organization promoting the interests of women-owned and minority-owned banking institutions. Founded in 1927, it provides information and resources to help banks create strong working relationships with corporations. Its website includes media presentations, a list of upcoming industry events, and other helpful information.

Controller

A controller is the head financial manager in a company. Although a controller's duties can vary depending on the size and makeup of the company, generally he or she provides financial leadership. Controllers can also be called comptrollers, treasurers, or financial managers.

A controller has many responsibilities. One of the most important is to produce financial reports. The controller examines all aspects of the company's accounting practices and financial activities and summarizes them in written reports or spreadsheets. These reports can have many different focuses, including creating a picture of the company's financial health, forecasting goals for the future, or examining market trends that could affect the company's financial performance. These reports are often in the form of complicated spreadsheets that provide specific information about many different financial aspects.

Controllers are also responsible for the business's accounting practices. The controller oversees all accounting activities and makes sure that all transactions are made and documented correctly. Depending on the size

At a Glance:
Controller

Minimum Educational Requirements
Bachelor's or master's degree

Personal Qualities
Strong analytical and math skills; good management skills; good at communicating with others

Certification and Licensing
Certification is not required but is preferred

Working Conditions
Indoors in an office

Salary Range
From $59,630 to $187,200

Number of Jobs
As of 2012 about 532,100

Future Job Outlook
Growth rate of 9 percent through 2022

and structure of the company, he or she may also oversee cash management, payments, payroll, bank statement reconciliation, and accounts payable and receivable functions. The controller may also supervise the accounting staff.

Establishing internal controls is another important function performed by a controller. Internal controls are a system of checks and balances that ensures that all financial procedures are honest and not fraudulent. A controller's responsibilities could include reviewing and approving invoices and signing checks.

Controllers must maintain knowledge of current policies, procedures, and financial laws. By doing this, the controller helps keep the company operating without fraud or other illegal financial activity. He or she is also responsible for working with tax accountants to prepare company income tax returns as well as outside auditors to check on the company's accounting practices. In order to perform these functions, a controller should keep excellent records and have them available for examination.

Controllers are responsible for creating many different reports. These reports can include financial statements, balance sheets, cash flow reports, and budgets. Controllers do not just report what is true about the company in the present day. They must also see into the future in order to prepare financial projections. These projections give suggestions on how a company's financial health may be affected by future trends and how the company can take steps to ensure healthy financial growth. These reports may help the controller advise his or her company about development opportunities that could increase profits or identify areas where financial improvement is needed. Although a company's chief financial officer may be the person who finalizes an organization's financial policies, he or she cannot do so without the controller's input. The controller is the one who identifies financial issues, assesses risk, analyzes efficiency, and suggests ways in which the company's financial policy can work successfully.

In the past, controllers spent much of their time preparing financial reports. However, new computer software has made it possible to quickly produce these reports. Because of this change in technology, a controller's role has grown to include data analysis and advising management on how to make strong financial decisions.

Controllers generally work in an office and spend most of their time in front of a computer. Controllers work in a large variety of industries, including banks, insurance agencies, and large corporations. They may also work for the government.

How Do You Become a Controller?

Education

Because a controller is a senior position, candidates are expected to have a great deal of education and experience. Although a candidate may begin his or her career with a bachelor's degree in finance, accounting, economics, or business administration, most employers look for a candidate who has a master's degree in one of these fields.

Certification and Licensing

Certification is not required to be a controller. However, many controllers do become certified in order to demonstrate their commitment and competence. Two of the most popular certifications are the chartered financial analyst (CFA) from the CFA Institute and the certified treasury professional from the Association for Financial Professionals. Both of these certifications require at least a bachelor's degree as well as several years of relevant work experience and passing an exam.

A controller's career might also be helped if he or she is a certified public accountant (CPA) or a certified management accountant (CMA). Becoming a CPA or CMA involves passing a difficult exam, but having this certification can help someone who is looking to advance in a financial career.

Volunteer Work and Internships

Anyone interested in becoming a controller should look for ways to gain experience in the accounting and finance fields. One way to do this is to undertake an internship. Many colleges and business schools can arrange internships with a variety of companies and financial institutions. Although these internships are often unpaid, they usually provide academic credits and are a great way to gain work experience. Internships are also a good way for a candidate to meet a network of professionals who may help him or her later on.

Similarly, people interested in a financial career can also look for volunteer work in their community. For example, a nonprofit organization or charity may be happy to have volunteers assist their accounting staff. Again, this is an excellent way to gain experience and meet other professionals in the industry.

Skills and Personality

Controllers must be able to pay close attention to detail. They must be able to follow financial trends and understand how they may affect a company's future performance. Controllers should also have excellent analytical skills because they are required to evaluate information and make decisions based on what they learn. They should also be able to solve problems and be able to make decisions quickly and confidently.

Excellent communication and organizational skills are also important. Controllers spend much of their time preparing forecasts and reports, so they must be able to communicate their evaluations and recommendations in a clear and understandable manner. Controllers should also be good team players and have good management and supervisory skills.

Computer skills are another valuable asset for this career. A controller must be able to read and understand complex financial documents, such as financial statements, spreadsheets, and market forecasts.

Controllers should also be organized. They deal with a large range of information and many different financial documents, and they must be able to gather information from these sources to create reports or share company information with auditors and tax accountants. It is very important that controllers know where to find the information they need without any difficulties.

It is also vital that controllers be ethical and honest. There are many rules and laws in the financial industry. Controllers must follow those rules in order to protect themselves, their staff, and their company from financial ruin and legal difficulties.

Employers

A controller can be employed by a corporation, business, or nonprofit organization. Controllers also work for banks, insurance companies, and the government. Generally, the larger the organization, the more specialized the controller's job will be. For example, a controller working for a smaller company might also handle accounting responsibilities, such as paying bills and collecting payments.

Working Conditions

Controllers often work long hours. They can expect to work more than forty hours per week. They generally work on a computer at a desk, although they may also spend time in meetings or business presentations. A controller who works for a company with a network of offices might travel to different locations to assess the financial health and direction of all parts of the corporation.

Earnings

The median annual salary for controllers was $109,740 in 2012. Controllers could expect a starting salary of approximately $59,630 in 2012. An experienced controller could earn up to $187,200.

Most controllers work full time and are paid a flat salary. They can expect to receive benefits such as paid vacation time and holidays, sick time, and health insurance. Large corporations may also offer other benefits, such as use of the company gym or payment of educational expenses.

Opportunities for Advancement

Controllers often enter the financial industry by working first as a loan officer, accountant, auditor, or financial analyst. Working in a bank, investment firm, or another finance-based industry is a good way to start. As a candidate gains more experience, he or she can move into management-level positions and eventually achieve the goal of becoming a controller. Acquiring certification can also help controllers advance to more challenging and well-paying positions, such as a company's chief financial officer.

What Is the Future Outlook for Controllers?

The Bureau of Labor Statistics estimates that the demand for controllers will grow about 9 percent through 2022, which is an average rate of growth. This rate would add about 47,100 new jobs within the decade.

The need for controllers and other financial managers should remain steady. Businesses and other organizations need strong financial leadership to survive, and there will always be a need for strong candidates who can interpret financial trends and help organizations achieve financial stability and growth. A candidate who can provide strong financial leadership is a key part of any successful business, and organizations will be looking for people who can meet this need both today and in the future.

Find Out More

Association for Financial Professionals (AFP)
4520 East-West Hwy., Suite 750
Bethesda, MD 20814
phone: (301) 907-2862
website: www.afponline.org

The AFP is the leading professional society for treasury and finance professionals around the world. It offers a certified treasury professional credential. This organization is also an excellent resource for career development and offers informational meetings and conferences on a number of topics.

CFA Institute
915 E. High St.
Charlottesville, VA 22902
phone: (800) 247-8132
website: www.cfainstitute.org

The CFA Institute provides education, professional development, and other resources to financial professionals, including many certification courses in areas such as investment decision making and strategy, portfolio and wealth management, financial planning, and risk management.

Chief Financial Officers Council
1800 F St. NW
Washington, DC 20405
phone: (844) 872-4681
website: https://cfo.gov

This government organization is dedicated to improving financial management in the US government. It also offers news events, a library of documents of interest to controllers and chief financial officers, and a job listing.

Government Finance Officers Association (GFOA)
203 N. LaSalle St., Suite 2700
Chicago, IL 60601
phone: (312) 977-9700
website: www.gfoa.org

The GFOA, founded in 1906, represents public finance officials in the United States and Canada. The goal of this organization is to aid its members in creating and implementing operations by providing resources on financial planning and policies that will benefit the public.

Economic Development Planner

What Does an Economic Development Planner Do?

At a Glance:

Economic Development Planner

Minimum Educational Requirements
Master's degree

Personal Qualities
Strong management and communication skills; good at working with others; good analytical and decision-making skills

Certification and Licensing
Some states require licenses

Working Conditions
In an office and out in the community

Salary Range
From $41,490 to $97,630

Number of Jobs
As of 2012, about 38,700

Future Job Outlook
Growth rate of 10 percent through 2022

Housing developments, shopping centers, and office buildings do not just go up by themselves. Building new construction takes years of planning. Long before the first shovelful of dirt is dug up, men and women work, often for years, in order to carefully plan construction that is acceptable to local governments and community members. Much of this planning involves financial considerations. That is where the job of an economic development planner comes in.

Economic development planners help develop plans and programs for the use of land. They study the economic impact of new construction, from how much it will cost to how much revenue, or income, it will provide. Economic development planners may work to bring new commercial activity to an area or diversify the activity that is there. Other goals include creating jobs, building new housing, or building facilities that will improve a community's quality of life.

Many communities are looking to attract more businesses in order to provide jobs for their residents and make their communities more desirable places to live. Communities may also want to create places that provide recreational facilities, such as parks, shopping malls, or sports arenas. Or they might want to improve their downtown by attracting new businesses or offering incentives to encourage businesses to remain in the area. These communities hire economic development planners to figure out how new businesses or attractions will affect the community's finances. For example, a business must pay taxes to the local government, so an economic planner would have to figure out how much the community could expect to receive in tax revenue. At the same time, the community might have to build new roads to accommodate a new sports arena, so the costs of building and maintaining those roads would also have to be figured out.

Often a developer comes into an area with a request to build a new housing development or shopping center. In this case, the local community's economic development planner would once again figure out the benefits and costs of permitting this new construction to take place. He or she would evaluate studies of similar projects and figure out how such a project might affect the area, then make recommendations as to what the best course of action would be.

Economic development planners might also assist local organizations or businesses in taking advantage of economic development opportunities such as grants or government aid to complete a specific project. They may work with local residents to develop economic partnerships with government agencies or businesses to create new opportunities.

Economic development planners do not work alone. Generally they are part of a team that includes other planners, such as urban and regional planners. All of these planners work together to ensure that all the facts, both good and bad, of a building project are spelled out clearly before construction begins. They identify community needs and develop short- and long-term plans to meet those needs. For example, an area might need a new school. It is up to the planners to find the best location for this school, decide how big it should be, and

Economic development planners discuss a land use proposal. As part of their job, they determine the economic impact of new construction such as housing developments, shopping centers, and office buildings. They might also help cities and counties attract new businesses.

work out all the economic elements that building a new school would involve. An economic development planner might focus on a large issue, such as attracting more businesses to a town, or on a smaller project, such as building one new shopping mall.

Economic development planners must work closely with the local community. Residents always have many questions about new construction and are often concerned about how that construction will affect their quality of life. Economic development planners gather information to answer those questions and create a clear picture of how development will affect an area.

Because economic development planners need to work with the community at large, they spend a great deal of time meeting with government officials, community members, and other groups to identify a community's needs, goals, and concerns. Planners use research and data analysis to create strategies that best meet the needs of everyone involved.

Economic development planners spend some of their time working in offices. In the office, much of their time is spent on a computer. Planners must create and update financial spreadsheets, conduct research, and investigate sources of funding, such as grants from the government or other organizations. Economic development planners also spend time in meetings with other members of their team.

Economic development planners also travel to building sites. They also attend community meetings, which may mean working during the evening or on weekends.

An economic development planner's job can be very stressful. New building projects or decisions on how to use land can face strong opinions and opposition from community members and local planning boards. Planners must answer difficult questions and provide information to meet the needs of everyone in a community. They must work with politicians, developers, and the public to find the plan that makes the best economic sense for a community. Economic development planners may also face tight deadlines in order to obtain legal permits or find sources for financing a project.

Most economic development planners work for the government. The US Bureau of Labor Statistics states that about 65 percent work in local government. Most of these jobs are found in large metropolitan areas, although suburban and rural areas also need economic development planners. Economic development planners also work for real estate developers, nonprofit organizations, consulting firms, and architectural and engineering firms.

How Do You Become an Economic Development Planner?

Education

Economic development planners should have a master's degree from a school that offers an urban or regional planning program. In 2013 seventy-two universities offered this type of program. Master's programs accept students with a wide variety of undergraduate degrees.

Most candidates have a bachelor's degree in economics, political science, environmental design, or engineering.

Most master's programs include several different components. Along with time in the classroom, a master's candidate in economic development planning would also spend time in the field or in seminars. The goal is to learn to solve problems, gather accurate information, and use that information to best determine the needs of a community and how to meet these needs.

There are currently fifteen schools that offer accredited bachelor's degree programs in planning. Someone with a bachelor's degree can qualify for a job as an assistant or junior planner. However, there are very few of these jobs available, and candidates should also have some work experience in public planning or public policy.

Certification and Licensing

As of 2012 New Jersey was the only state that required planners to be licensed. Michigan also requires candidates to register with the state in order to be called *community planners*. However, becoming certified can increase opportunities to advance in this field and prove to employers that the planner is serious about this career. The American Institute of Certified Planners offers a professional certification. Candidates must meet certain education and experience requirements and pass an exam. This certification must be renewed every two years.

Volunteer Work and Internships

Although it is difficult to find volunteer work as an economic development planner, students can gain experience through internships with a local government or planning board. Many master's programs provide internship opportunities during the summer or after the student completes his or her degree.

Skills and Personality

Economic development planners should have strong analytical skills. They use these skills when they analyze information from various sources, such as censuses, tax records, and other data.

Economic development planners should also have strong decision-making skills because they will be asked to provide suggestions based on economic data. They should also be able to solve problems and be confident in their abilities.

Excellent communication and organizational skills are also important. Economic development planners often must prepare research reports, write grant proposals, create spreadsheets, and then share these reports with others. Planners must be able to communicate their evaluations and recommendations and cite specific details to back up their findings. Much of an economic development planner's time is spent meeting with government and community officials who will want to know exactly how new development will impact the community.

Computer skills are another valuable asset for an economic development planner. He or she will be asked to read and understand complex financial documents and use computer software to make predictions about economic trends.

Because they work closely with other planners, officials, and corporate representatives, economic development planners should also be good team players and be able to work well with a variety of different personalities.

On the Job

Employers

Two-thirds of all economic development planners are employed by the government. Many work for cities or large towns. Planners may also find employment with real estate development companies, non-profit organizations, or consulting firms.

Working Conditions

Economic development planners generally work full time during normal business hours. They may be expected to work evenings or weekends in order to attend community meetings. Some overtime may also be required.

Economic development planners can expect to work in an office setting. They generally work on computers and may also do a lot of business over the phone. In addition, planners will attend many meetings, both in and out of the office, and may need to visit building sites on occasion.

Earnings

The median annual salary for an economic development planner was $65,230 in 2012. That same year economic development planners could expect a starting salary of about $41,490. An experienced planner could earn more than $97,630.

Most economic development planners are paid a flat salary. Full-time employees can also expect to receive benefits such as paid vacation time and holidays, sick time, and health insurance.

Opportunities for Advancement

Economic development planners can get started in this field by finding a position as a junior planner or as an assistant to a planner already working in the field. As planners gain more experience, they will be able to advance in the field. Obtaining more education and certification will also help a planner find better job opportunities.

A willingness to relocate for work can also help an economic development planner's career. A planner who is able to move to a different state to fill a job opportunity will find more chances to advance in this career.

What Is the Future Outlook for Economic Development Planners?

The Bureau of Labor Statistics estimates that the demand for economic development planners will grow about 10 percent through 2022, which is an average rate of growth. This rate would add about four thousand new jobs.

Many factors determine the need for economic development planners. When communities and developers have funds for development projects, there is a higher demand for planners. There may also be more government funding available for new projects during these conditions. There is a much smaller demand, as well as more competition, during an economic downturn or recession.

However, after economic conditions improve, there is often an upsurge in the number of building projects as developers and government officials carry out projects that had been put off during the poor economy. When these projects get started, economic development planners will be needed to help plan, oversee, and carry out the projects. The need for more economic development planners may also grow as the population increases. These increases create more demand for housing, schools, entertainment facilities, and other community projects.

Find Out More

American Institute of Certified Planners (AICP)
205 N. Michigan Ave., Suite 1200
Chicago, IL 60601
phone: (312) 431-9100
website: www.planning.org/aicp

The AICP is the professional institute of the American Planning Association. It offers certification, community programs, and professional development opportunities to economic development planners and other urban and regional planners.

American Planning Association (APA)
205 N. Michigan Ave., Suite 1200
Chicago, IL 60601
phone: (312) 431-9100
website: www.planning.org

The APA "works to make great communities happen" by bringing together urban and economic development planners, community leaders, and government officials. Founded in 1978, the APA is a not-for-profit educational organization offering scholarships, community programs, and ethical guidance to planners and other professionals in the field.

International Economic Development Council (IEDC)
734 Fifteenth St. NW, Suite 900
Washington, DC 20005
phone: (202) 223-7800
website: www.iedconline.org

The IEDC's members are involved in economic development work around the world, benefiting many different types of communities. This organization provides leadership, networking opportunities, professional development, and public policy updates.

National Association of Development Organizations (NADO)
400 North Capitol St. NW, Suite 390
Washington, DC 20001
phone: (202) 624-7806
website: www.nado.org

NADO provides advocacy, research, education, and training for regional development agencies across the United States. Its website provides a wealth of information and news to assist regional planners to create and build community projects.

Financial Analyst

What Does a Financial Analyst Do?

Finances can be very complicated. When people and businesses invest their money, they want to make smart decisions that will result in earning money, not losing money. Financial analysts help people and businesses make investment decisions. They do this by assessing the performance of stocks, bonds, and other investments.

Financial analysts must be experts on the economy and the various financial markets. A financial analyst needs to know which investments are good and which ones should be avoided. He or she must constantly seek out updated information in order to present the best recommendations to clients.

Financial analysts study historical data about investment performance, but they also keep current and understand how a particular investment is performing now and how it may perform in the future. Analysts obtain this information by studying business and economic trends as well as studying specific companies' financial statements, value, and performance. They monitor developments in

At a Glance:
Financial Analyst

Minimum Educational Requirements
Bachelor's degree

Personal Qualities
Excellent critical-thinking and problem-solving skills; excellent communication skills; detail oriented and organized

Certification and Licensing
A financial analyst license and other financial certifications are recommended

Working Conditions
Indoors in an office

Salary Range
From $60,010 to $106,470

Number of Jobs
As of 2012 about 253,000

Future Job Outlook
Growth rate of 15 to 21 percent through 2022

many different fields, including increasingly important industries such as technology. Analysts use the information they gather to make predictions on how a particular investment might perform.

Most financial analysts fall into one of two categories: buy-side analysts and sell-side analysts. Buy-side analysts develop investment strategies for companies that have a large amount of money to invest. These companies include mutual funds, hedge funds, insurance companies, independent money managers, and some nonprofit organizations. Other financial analysts work as sell-side analysts. These analysts advise agents who sell stocks, bonds, and other investments to corporations or individual investors.

A financial analyst's focus is usually very specific. Agents focus on a specific industry, geographical area, or type of product. For example, an analyst may focus on the energy industry or on investments in Asia.

There are several areas on which financial analysts can focus. Some analysts work as portfolio managers. A portfolio is a collection of investments held by an individual or a company. Portfolio managers select the mix of investments that will work best for a specific portfolio. These investments can include different products, corporations, industries, and geographical regions.

Fund managers work exclusively with hedge funds or mutual funds. A hedge fund is a small partnership of investors that uses high-risk methods in hopes of earning a large return on their investment. A mutual fund is an investment program that includes different holdings in hopes of earning money for investors.

Other analysts study specific companies and investments. A ratings analyst evaluates the ability of companies or governments to pay their debts. This analysis can impact an organization's creditworthiness or its ability to pay debts and be financially secure. Risk analysts evaluate the risk in investment decisions and figure out how to limit losses.

Financial analysts work in offices. Many of them work in large financial institutions, such as investment firms, banks, or insurance agencies located in major cities like New York. Most financial analysts work full time and may often work more than forty hours a week. The *U.S. News & World Report* website states that one in three analysts puts in between fifty and seventy hours in an average workweek.

A typical day could include researching trends or companies by reading reports, gathering information, or meeting with representatives; writing reports explaining the analyst's recommendations; meeting with clients to discuss their portfolios; and studying the latest trends in the stock and bond markets.

Meeting with others is an important part of a financial analyst's job. He or she meets with clients to discover investment opportunities. Analysts also meet with potential businesses that are offering these opportunities. In addition, financial analysts often work in teams at their jobs, so meetings with colleagues are an important part of their day-to-day work environment.

How Do You Become a Financial Analyst?

Education

Financial analysts typically hold a bachelor's degree. This degree is usually in a field such as finance, accounting, or business. An understanding of how to read and evaluate accounting and financial statements is especially valuable. Some firms prefer to hire analysts who have a master's degree in finance or business administration.

Certification and Licensing

Many financial analysts choose to become certified financial analysts by completing certification and licensing programs. The Financial Industry Regulatory Authority (FINRA) is the main licensing organization for the securities industry. FINRA requires licenses for many financial analyst positions.

Certification is an excellent way to improve the chances of advancement. One certification is the chartered financial analyst (CFA) credential offered by the CFA Institute. Requirements for a CFA certification include a bachelor's degree, four years of work experience, and a passing grade on three different exams.

Becoming certified and licensed can increase opportunities to advance in this field and prove to employers that the financial analyst is serious about this career. Employers often sponsor certification programs and cover the costs for their employees. Most licensing programs require sponsorship by an employer as well.

Volunteer Work and Internships

Someone who is looking for a career as a financial analyst can look for volunteer work or internships in the financial industry. These positions not only provide experience but also can be an excellent way to network and meet new contacts who can help provide job opportunities in the future. As Manisha Thakor, founder and CEO of MoneyZen Wealth Management, explained on the *U.S. News & World Report* website, "Something as basic as offering to work with an established financial professional for five to ten hours a month can make all the difference. Remember to keep one hand in the books and one hand out shaking new ones."

Skills and Personality

Financial analysts must be able to pay close attention to detail. They must be able to follow trends and understand how they affect future performance in financial markets. Analysts should also have excellent critical-thinking skills because they are required to evaluate information and make decisions based on what they learn. They should also be able to solve problems and be able to make decisions quickly and confidently.

Excellent communication and organizational skills are also important. Financial analysts must be able to communicate their evaluations and recommendations to clients clearly and with specific detail. Much of their time is spent meeting with potential investors or with company officials to understand the value of a corporation's assets and the corporation's value in the market.

Computer skills are another valuable asset for a financial analyst. An analyst also must be able to read and understand complex financial documents, such as financial statements, investment prospectuses (documents that explain the terms of an investment), and corporate spreadsheets.

Financial analysts should also be confident in themselves. Analysts offer advice that can have a huge effect on the financial security of an individual or business. An analyst must be confident that his or her recommendations are good ones and be sure that he or she accurately interprets financial data to make intelligent decisions.

It is also vital that financial analysts know the rules of the financial industry. There are often strict regulations in place to protect investors, and financial analysts must be aware of these rules in order to make sure all recommendations are legal.

On the Job

Employers

Most financial analysts work for financial institutions such as banks, investment firms, or insurance agencies. Others may work for smaller companies within these fields. Most large financial institutions are located in large cities.

Working Conditions

Financial analysts can expect to work full time or even more than forty hours per week. Because much of their time can be spent in meetings, analysts often do their research after office hours. Their work is done at a desk in an office, although an analyst might use a laptop computer to research markets outside of the office as well.

Financial analysts may spend long hours in front of a computer or reading financial reports. They also spend a lot of time on the telephone talking to both investors and representatives offering investment opportunities.

Earnings

The median annual salary for financial analysts was $76,950 in 2012, and they could expect a starting salary of about $60,010. An experienced analyst could earn up to $106,470.

Most financial analysts are paid a flat salary. Full-time employees can also expect to receive benefits such as paid vacation time and holidays, sick time, and health insurance. Large corporations may also offer other benefits, such as use of the company gym or payment of educational expenses.

Opportunities for Advancement

Financial analysts can enter the field by obtaining a beginning position as a junior analyst. Junior analysts usually specialize in a specific field, such as mutual funds. As they gain more experience they can look for different areas of expertise and move up the ladder to a senior analyst position.

Financial analysts with more experience can become portfolio managers or fund managers. These positions require analysts to select a mix of different investments and recommend a more diversified strategy for investors to earn money. Acquiring certification or a specialized license can also help analysts advance to more challenging positions.

What Is the Future Outlook for Financial Analysts?

The Bureau of Labor Statistics estimates that the demand for financial analysts will grow about 16 percent through 2022, which is faster than the average rate of growth. This rate would add more than thirty-nine thousand new jobs within the decade.

The need for financial analysts should remain strong as more people and companies look to earn money through investments. Because financial markets can change quickly and seesaw wildly between gains and losses, many people need an experienced analyst to help them make important investment decisions. As the economy strengthens and individuals have more money to invest, the need for financial analysts will grow.

Demand for financial analysts should also become stronger because of the many new businesses entering the market. As more and more people choose to become entrepreneurs and start their own businesses, there will be an increased need for them to finance their business. Many companies do this by going public, or offering shares of stock to the public. It is up to financial analysts to determine if buying stock in a particular company is a smart investment choice and communicate this information to clients. Financial analysts can also advise businesses on how to offer stock and other investment options in the best way possible to give the business a good chance to succeed.

Find Out More

Association for Financial Professionals (AFP)
4520 East-West Hwy., Suite 750
Bethesda, MD 20814
phone: (301) 907-2862
website: www.afponline.org

The AFP is the leading professional society for treasury and finance professionals around the world. It offers a certified treasury professional credential. This organization is also an excellent resource for career development and offers informational meetings and conferences on a number of topics.

CFA Institute
915 E. High St.
Charlottesville, VA 22902
phone: (800) 247-8132
website: www.cfainstitute.org

The CFA Institute provides education, professional development, and other resources to financial professionals, including many certification courses in areas such as investment decision making and strategy, portfolio and wealth management, financial planning, and risk management.

Financial Industry Regulatory Authority (FINRA)
1735 K St.
Washington, DC 20006
phone: (301) 590-6500
website: www.finra.org

FINRA is an independent, not-for-profit organization dedicated to protecting investors and ensuring the integrity of the financial market through regulation. Its goal is for the market to operate fairly and honestly. FINRA runs the FINRA Investor Education Foundation to offer skills training and tools for individuals to achieve financial success as well as licensing programs, online and university classes, and conferences for financial analysts and other industry professionals.

New York Society of Security Analysts (NYSSA)
1540 Broadway, Suite 1010
New York, NY 10036
phone: (212) 541-4530
website: www.nyssa.org

NYSSA has been a leading organization for the investment community since 1937. It helps its members to uphold high ethical standards. Its website includes information on certification programs, professional networking, and research and outreach opportunities for students.

Loan Officer

People take out loans to fulfill many different dreams. They may be financing a college education, buying a new house or car, or looking for money to start a new business. People visit loan officers to borrow money in order to fulfill these dreams. Loan officers help their clients apply for loans. They also determine the best type of loan for the situation and the amount of money their clients are qualified to borrow.

Loan officers usually specialize in one of three major branches: commercial, consumer, or mortgage. A commercial loan provides money to businesses. Commercial loans are usually more complicated than other types of loans. Commercial loans can also be for very large amounts. Sometimes these amounts are so large that several banks will work together to provide the entire amount. In this case, loan officers will work with multiple banks to put together one or more loans for the business client.

Consumer lenders provide loans to individuals. These individuals, or consumers, take out loans for major expenses such as paying for education, buy-

At a Glance:
Loan Officer

Minimum Educational Requirements
Bachelor's degree

Personal Qualities
Excellent people skills; excellent communication skills; good salesperson

Certification and Licensing
Mortgage loan originator license

Working Conditions
Indoors in an office or out in the community

Salary Range
About $32,600 to $119,710

Number of Jobs
As of 2012 about 297,000

Future Job Outlook
Growth rate of 8 percent through 2022

ing a house or an automobile, or taking on a project such as a home renovation.

Mortgage lending includes loans to individuals for buying homes or other real estate. Mortgage loans are also made to those seeking to purchase commercial properties, such as when an individual or group hopes to buy a building to use as a store, office, or other business location. Mortgage loan officers can work for banks or other lending institutions. These loan officers usually work closely with real estate agents who will refer prospective home buyers or property buyers to the loan officer to arrange their mortgage.

Many loan officers work for banks, credit unions, and other financial institutions. When a bank makes a loan, it charges interest. That interest is how the bank makes money. Because of this, a large part of a loan officer's job is to determine if a client is creditworthy—that is, if the client will be able to pay off the loan and the interest in a specified period of time. If a client does not pay off the loan, the bank loses its money. That is why it is important for a loan officer to be sure a client will be able to repay the loan. Loan officers do this by using analytical and mathematical formulas to determine a client's monthly income and what percentage of that income is needed to repay the loan and the interest.

Loan officers are also salespeople. Many loan officers actively look for clients in order to earn money. The loan officer's company will earn money by charging interest on the loans it offers to clients. Loan officers match their client's needs with the best loan opportunities, looking for reasonable interest rates and repayment schedules. An independent loan officer might work with the support of a broker to offer many different services to the client, such as advising the client about the best loans available, gathering documentation for the loan application, and communicating with the loan underwriter or bank to make sure the loan is approved.

Loan officers in the commercial and consumer markets usually work a forty-hour week from an office in a bank or other institution. A mortgage loan officer often works longer hours, including nights and weekends. He or she may also meet with clients outside of the office, traveling to their homes or workplaces in order to work out the terms of a loan.

A loan officer's day can include many different duties. Some of their job responsibilities include contacting companies or people to ask if they need a loan and explaining different types of loans to applicants. Loan officers also meet with loan applicants to answer questions and gather information. They must obtain and verify financial information, such as the client's credit rating and sources of income. In addition to selling loans, some loan officers act as underwriters. Underwriters analyze the applicant's finances to decide if he or she qualifies for a loan. This process can be done by using formulas and calculations or by using underwriting software that quickly issues an analysis and recommendation. Finally, the loan officer may approve a loan application or refer it to a manager with a recommendation on a final decision.

One of the advantages of being a loan officer is the ability to make decisions without waiting for someone else's approval. A loan officer uses guidelines and formulas to decide if a loan is going to work, but he or she is also able to make loans based on his or her own analysis of a client's situation. Loan officers also have the pleasure of really making a difference in their clients' lives and helping clients achieve important life goals. For many clients, buying a house or sending a child to college is the fulfillment of a lifelong dream, and the loan officer becomes an important part of making that dream come true.

However, loan officers also face the unpleasant task of rejecting loan applicants who do not meet the requirements. Loan officers may also have to deal with clients who can no longer fulfill their loan obligations and have fallen behind in their payments. Loan officers who work for a commission or who have high quotas (a certain number of loans they are expected to make in a specific time period) may also feel intense pressure or stress as they struggle to earn more business.

How Do You Become a Loan Officer?

Education

Loan officers typically hold a bachelor's degree. This degree is usually in a related field such as finance or business. Commercial loan officers analyze the finances of a business applying for a loan, so an understanding of general accounting and financial statements is especially valuable. Some firms prefer to hire loan officers who have a master's degree in business administration.

Certification and Licensing

Mortgage loan officers must have a mortgage loan originator (MLO) license. To become licensed, loan officers must complete twenty hours of classwork, pass an exam, and have background and credit checks. An MLO license must be renewed every year. Some states have additional requirements for mortgage loan officers.

Several schools and banking associations, such as the American Bankers Association and the Mortgage Bankers Association, offer certification courses for loan officers. Although certification is not required, obtaining certification shows an employer that the loan officer is dedicated and willing to go the extra mile to be a high performer.

Volunteer Work and Internships

Someone who is looking for a career as a loan officer can look for volunteer work or internships in the banking industry or in sales or customer service. Work experience in these fields is also an advantage in preparing for a career as a loan officer.

Skills and Personality

The best loan officers have excellent communication and sales skills. Many are paid on commission, which means the more loans they arrange, the more money they earn. Frank Donnelly, former president of the Mortgage Bankers Association of Metropolitan Washington, told *U.S. News & World Report*'s website that loan officers need "to be detail-oriented because loans today have so many data elements. You need to be good at following up, at communicating with your clients . . . and you need discipline."

Excellent people skills are a must for a career as a loan officer. A loan officer deals with many different types of clients. The loan officer seeks out clients to sell a product to them, but the officer must also understand their clients' needs and work with them to obtain the best loan for their situation.

A loan officer also needs to communicate with managers and underwriters to make it clear that their clients have the necessary income and financial background to be good candidates for the loan. Loan officers also need to be detail oriented and very organized in order to keep track of the many details any loan application requires.

Computer skills are another valuable asset for a loan officer. Loan officers often use mortgage and banking software to determine if a client is qualified to take out a loan.

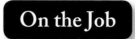

On the Job

Employers

Most loan officers work for commercial banks, credit unions, mortgage companies, or other financial institutions.

Working Conditions

Loan officers can expect to work full time or at least thirty-five hours per week. Many mortgage loan officers work even longer hours; they often meet with clients after regular business hours. "You have to be prepared to work the hours when your clients aren't working," says Donnelly. "That means working at night or on weekends."

Loan officers generally work at a desk in an office. They spend a great deal of time on the telephone and working on a computer. A loan officer should also be comfortable working face to face with clients.

Earnings

The median annual salary for loan officers was $59,820 in 2012. A loan officer could expect a starting salary of about $32,600 in 2012, and an experienced loan officer could earn up to $119,710.

There are several different methods used to pay loan officers. Some employers pay their loan officers by commission. A commission can be a percentage of the sale or a flat rate paid for each sale. Employers use commissions to encourage workers to produce more loans. Other employers pay a flat salary. Or an employer may pay a worker with a combination of salary and commissions.

Full-time loan officers can also expect to receive benefits along with their salaries. These benefits include health insurance; paid vacation, holiday, and sick time; and retirement benefits.

Opportunities for Advancement

Once a loan officer has gained experience, he or she can move to larger bank branches or financial institutions. He or she may be given the responsibility of handling more loans and business transactions. Loan officers can also move up to managerial positions. A manager supervises other loan officers and staff. Managers can also have more responsibilities when it comes to making decisions on whether to offer a loan.

What Is the Future Outlook for Loan Officers?

The Bureau of Labor Statistics (BLS) estimates that the demand for loan officers will grow about 8 percent through 2022. This rate would add almost twenty-three thousand jobs within the decade. That is an average rate of growth.

The need for loan officers changes as the economy changes. When economic growth is strong and interest rates are low, more people take out loans. In that situation, the demand for loan officers increases. However, during a downturn in the economy, people are less willing to borrow money, and banks and other institutions are less willing to lend. That scenario creates less demand for loan officers.

The use of loan underwriting software may also limit job growth. Underwriting software can complete and approve (or reject) a loan in a short period of time and eliminate the need for a human loan officer. However, many financial institutions still use loan officers to check software results. This is especially true with complicated loans, such as commercial loans or large mortgages.

The BLS states that prospects for loan officers should improve over the next decade as the economy recovers from the recession that ended in 2009. During the recession, many individuals put off borrowing money, and companies put off borrowing funds to improve or expand their business. As the economy gets better, people and companies are more willing to borrow, and banks are more willing to lend. This should create more job opportunities for people with banking, lending, and sales experience. Networking can also increase a loan officer's chances of employment; officers who have established contacts and working relationships will find more opportunity in the industry.

Find Out More

American Bankers Association (ABA)
1120 Connecticut Ave. NW
Washington, DC 20036
phone: (800) 226-5377
website: www.aba.com

The ABA calls itself "the voice of the $15 trillion banking industry." It offers resources to banking professionals, such as certification programs, job listings, and informational programs and tools.

Integrity Mortgage Licensing
3420 Bristol St., Suite 621
Costa Mesa, CA 92626
phone: (714) 721-3963
website: www.integritymortgagelicensing.com

Integrity Mortgage Licensing is a mortgage licensing service that assists loan officers in meeting state licensing requirements. Its website includes many resources, including information on obtaining an MLO license as well as specific state-by-state requirements for loan officers.

Mortgage Bankers Association (MBA)
1919 M St. NW, 5th Floor
Washington, DC 20036
phone: (202) 557-2700
website: www.mba.org

The MBA includes all parts of the real estate finance industry, including loan originators, servicers, underwriters, compliance personnel, and information technology professionals. The MBA offers mortgage loan certification courses and other resources for loan officers and other real estate finance professionals.

Nationwide Mortgage Licensing System and Registry
phone: (855) 665-7123
website: http://mortgage.nationwidelicensingsystem.org

This resource center provides users with tools, tips, news, and updates regarding the mortgage loan industry. The center features workshops and other events. It also provides information on certification and state licensing requirements.

Personal Financial Adviser

What Does a Personal Financial Adviser Do?

At a Glance:

Personal Financial Adviser

Minimum Educational Requirements
Bachelor's degree

Personal Qualities
Excellent customer and personal service skills; knowledge of economics and accounting; strong sales and marketing skills

Certification and Licensing
Some states require licensing; certification is also recommended

Working Conditions
Indoors in an office

Salary Range
From $33,190 to $187,199

Number of Jobs
As of 2012 about 223,400

Future Job Outlook
Growth rate of 27 percent through 2022

Life is full of important financial decisions. People need to know what investments will earn the most money, how much money they should save for retirement, how much life insurance to purchase, and how to avoid costly tax mistakes, among other vital decisions. However, making important financial decisions can be complicated, difficult, or just downright scary. That is where personal financial advisers (also known as personal financial planners) enter the picture. A personal financial adviser's job is to give advice and help people make the best financial decisions.

Becoming a personal financial adviser is a relatively new career option. In the past bankers, stockbrokers, or insurance agents helped people make financial decisions. However, since the 1990s, finances have become so complicated that many people saw a new opportunity and created a whole new career. As James Kinney, a certified financial planner and founder of the firm Financial Pathways, explains to the *U.S. News & World Report* website, "As a larger portion of the industry shifts away from the banks, brokers, and insurance companies, additional opportunities have opened."

Financial advisers may play many different roles and have many different responsibilities. Advisers may sit down with clients and counsel them about financial decisions, such as saving enough money for a child's college education or paying back credit card debt. To do this, a financial adviser might assess what goals are most important to the client and help him or her set up a budget to meet those goals. These goals might be short term, such as paying for a wedding, or long term, such as funding a child's education or paying for retirement.

Other financial advisers focus on guiding clients to prepare for the future. Many people worry about having enough money to enjoy a comfortable retirement. Personal financial advisers work with clients to create a savings and investment plan with the goal of providing enough money to pay for future needs. Financial advisers can also assist clients with preparing for expenses that arise because of illness, disability, or death. They may recommend and sell insurance policies that provide assistance in case of long-term medical care or a life insurance policy that pays a certain amount if a family member passes away.

Personal financial advisers may work in an office, but they also may spend a large amount of their time meeting with clients outside of the office. During these meetings advisers discuss financial goals and explain different financial services and options. They educate clients about different investment options and the benefits and risks each option involves. They may recommend specific investments or create an overall financial plan that will help the client meet his or her goals. Although many financial advisers provide guidance for a wide range of topics, others specialize in specific areas, such as retirement planning or insurance.

Setting up investment accounts is often a large part of a personal financial adviser's responsibilities. After the adviser and the client determine the best investments, the adviser is responsible for purchasing those investments and setting up a portfolio. Once an investment account is created, the adviser should monitor the account to make sure

A personal financial adviser offers information and perspective to help clients make good financial decisions concerning investments, retirement options, reducing debt, and planning college education for their children. Strong analytical and interpersonal skills are essential for this job.

it is performing up to expectations. If the account is not performing well, the adviser might meet with the client to discuss other investment options, then reinvest the money according to the client's wishes.

Personal financial advisers need to be good salespeople. They need to convince clients to buy their services. Although some financial advisers are employed by banks, insurance agencies, or brokerage firms (companies that sell stocks and bonds as investments), most advisers work for themselves. To find clients, personal financial advisers have to spend a lot of time on networking and marketing. They may host dinners, seminars, and informational meetings where they explain the services they offer. Personal financial advisers also rely on networking in order to meet new clients and spread the word about the services they offer.

Along with providing guidance and advice, many personal financial advisers buy and sell stocks, bonds, insurance, and other financial products. To do this, advisers must be licensed. Obtaining a license involves passing a course that includes a rigorous exam.

Although many personal financial advisers work with clients who have average financial resources, wealth managers work with people who have a lot of money to invest. Wealth managers act as personal bankers for their clients. They manage large collections of investments and usually work with a team of financial professionals, including accountants and financial analysts, to handle their clients' money.

How Do You Become a Personal Financial Adviser?

Education

Personal financial advisers typically start with a bachelor's degree in a field such as finance, accounting, economics, or business. Some colleges now offer a bachelor's degree in financial planning. Most advisers go on to obtain a master's degree and certification in order to advance in this career. Courses in insurance, estate planning, tax law, and risk management are also helpful.

Certification and Licensing

Personal financial advisers who buy or sell stocks, bonds, or insurance policies must be licensed. The type of license needed depends on the product the adviser sells. Many advisers are licensed to sell more than one product. Personal financial advisers who sell insurance need licenses issued by state insurance boards. In addition, investment firms must register with state regulators, and large firms must register with the Securities and Exchange Commission, a federal agency that regulates markets and enforces government rules regarding the buying and selling of stocks and other securities.

In addition to obtaining licenses, personal financial advisers may also choose to become certified. Certifications can improve an adviser's reputation and make him or her more appealing to new clients or employers. One popular certification is the certified financial planner (CFP). To obtain this certification, advisers must have a bachelor's degree and at least three years of experience in the financial world. The adviser must also follow a code of ethics and pass an exam that covers such topics as risk management, insurance, retirement planning, debt management, and investment and real estate planning.

Personal financial advisers may also take exams such as the Series 63, Series 65, and Series 66 exams to meet state regulatory requirements. These exams are given by the North American Securities Administrators Association.

Volunteer Work and Internships

Someone who is investigating a career as a personal financial adviser may choose to do volunteer work or internships in the financial industry. These positions not only provide experience but also can be an excellent way to network. In addition, they will allow prospective financial advisers to learn from more experienced people in the field and perhaps find a mentor to help further their career.

Skills and Personality

Personal financial advisers must have strong analytical skills. These skills allow the adviser to determine what the best investments for a client are. Advisers must be able to understand and process a large amount of information, including risk, economic trends, and regulatory and legal issues. Personal financial advisers should also be good at math since they will be working with numbers and formulas every day.

Good interpersonal skills are a must for this career. A major part of a financial adviser's job is making clients feel comfortable. It is unlikely that a client will invest money with an adviser he or she does not trust. Advisers must also be able to answer clients' questions and make sure they understand any risk or consequences of investing. In a blog post on Freefinancialadvising.blogspot.com, Eric Schaefer of the wealth management and financial planning firm Savant Capital insists that he and his colleagues "agree that 80 percent of our job is psychology and only 20 percent is financial. . . . The ability to understand the core concerns and goals of a client or prospective client is much more valuable" than business or economic knowledge.

Excellent communication and organizational skills are also important. Financial advisers meet with clients every day and must be able to explain complicated financial matters in a way clients will understand. In addition, personal financial advisers must be good at selling their services and themselves. Persistence, confidence, and an upbeat personality are valuable assets in this career.

It is also vital that financial advisers know the rules of the financial industry. There are many legal and regulatory requirements involved in selling investments, and advisers must follow these rules in order to guide their clients and keep these clients—and the advisers themselves—out of serious trouble.

On the Job

Employers

While some personal financial advisers work for banks, insurance firms, or other financial companies, many more are self-employed. They set up their own businesses and are responsible for finding clients and providing them with the best investment opportunities.

Working Conditions

Financial advisers can expect to work full time. In addition to their work during the day, they may also meet with clients in the evening or on weekends. Advisers generally work in an office and spend long hours in front of a computer. They also spend a lot of time on the telephone or going to community events in order to find new clients.

Earnings

Personal financial advisers can make an excellent salary. In 2012 the median annual salary for financial advisers was $67,520. However, many advisers earn much more. According to the website *U.S. News & World Report*, top advisers earned more than $187,199 in 2013. However, starting salaries are much lower, in the $30,000 range.

In addition to their salaries, advisers who work for companies may also earn large bonuses. The best-paid advisers live in areas with strong financial industries—such as Bridgeport, Connecticut; Wilmington, Delaware; and Greenville, North Carolina—as well as major cities such as New York and Los Angeles.

Personal financial advisers who work for companies can also expect to receive benefits such as health insurance, paid vacations, and sick time. However, advisers who are self-employed or run their own small business have a more difficult time obtaining these types of benefits.

Opportunities for Advancement

Although financial advisers generally need just a bachelor's degree to start their career, obtaining a master's degree in finance is usually required to advance. In addition, personal financial advisers will benefit from becoming certified and licensed to sell different financial products. As advisers gain more knowledge and experience, they may be offered higher positions within a financial organization, or they may decide they have enough knowledge to start their own business.

Some companies, such as Wells Fargo Advisers, hire trainees and send them to a thirty-one-week program that includes obtaining necessary licenses. After the training period ends, students are given positions as junior advisers and are expected to find new clients. Over time an adviser can move up in the Wells Fargo organization, gaining more clients and responsibilities, and earning a lot more money.

What Is the Future Outlook for Personal Financial Advisers?

Personal financial advisers are expected to be one of the fastest-growing occupations over the next decade. The Bureau of Labor Statistics estimates that the demand for financial advisers will grow by 27 percent through 2022, which is much faster than average. This rate would add 60,300 new jobs within the decade.

The need for personal financial advisers should remain strong as large numbers of people face the need to plan for life-changing events. As the population ages, there is a greater need for planning retirement or long-term medical care. In addition, most businesses no longer offer pensions (an annual payment to retired workers), leaving people to invest and manage money on their own. Because financial planning can be so complicated, there is a greater need for personal financial advisers to help.

Find Out More

Certified Financial Planner Board of Standards
1425 K St. NW, #800
Washington, DC 20005
phone: (800) 487-1497
website: www.cfp.net

The Certified Financial Planner Board of Standards is a nonprofit organization that acts in the public interest to establish professional standards for those in the financial industry. It offers a number of certifications and other educational and professional opportunities.

College for Financial Planning
9000 E. Nichols Ave., Suite 200
Centennial, CO 80112
phone: (800) 237-9990
website: www.cffp.edu

The College for Financial Planning offers classes for many different levels of financial professions. Classes include several certification and licensing exams. The college's website also provides webinars and articles on information relevant to the financial planning community.

Financial Planning Association (FPA)
7535 E. Hampden Ave., Suite 600
Denver, CO 80231
phone: (800) 322-4900
website: www.onefpa.org

The FPA is the premier association for certified financial planners. The organization offers a number of educational opportunities as well as opportunities for networking and professional advancement.

North American Securities Administrators Association (NASAA)
750 First St. NE, Suite 1140
Washington, DC 20002
phone: (202) 737-0900
website: www.nasaa.org

The goal of this organization is to protect investors from fraud. NASAA licenses financial professionals, reviews financial transactions, promotes investor education, and enforces state laws. Its website also offers information about the Series 63, Series 65, and Series 66 licensing exams.

US Securities and Exchange Commission (SEC)
SEC Headquarters
100 F St. NE
Washington, DC 20549
phone: (202) 942-8088
website: www.sec.gov

The SEC is a government agency whose mission is to protect investors and maintain orderly markets. It does this by setting laws for the financial industry and investigating fraud. The SEC is a valuable resource for financial advisers and anyone seeking to learn more about how the US financial system operates.

Interview with an Accountant

Mary Louise Moore is an accountant for Software Services in Bellevue, Washington. She has worked as an accountant for more than thirty years. She answered questions about her career by e-mail.

Q: Why did you become an accountant?
A: I took an accounting course in college and, right from the start, it came easily to me. It was logical and balanced, like algebra. It just appealed to me. Note that not everyone will feel this way. There were quite a few people in the accounting course who were completely lost, and some people do not have the patience for the attention to detail that the job requires. But I loved it.

Q: What type of company do you work for? What are some of your job responsibilities?
A: Software Services is a small academic software reseller. I am responsible for cash receipts and payments, credit and collections, bank reconciliations, and payroll. I also maintain the general ledger (a master list of all of the company's accounting transactions) and file all monthly and quarterly payroll tax returns.

Q: Can you describe your typical workday?
A: I set up a calendar of due dates for things like payroll and taxes, and I also schedule one day a week to pay other bills that are due. The first order of the day is to look at the calendar to see what I have to do that day. Then I deal with any mail that comes in, such as cash receipts, new bills, etc. If the sales department has a new customer, I do a credit check. If existing customers are late with payments, I make collection calls.

Q: What do you like most about your job?

A: By its nature, accounting is not as subjective and dependent on other people's opinions as a lot of other professions. For example, say you are a salesperson or any kind of creative artist. You could have the best idea in the world, but if other people don't agree with you and support you, your idea will likely not come to fruition. Or you could try something, and it could fail for political or other reasons, resulting in a lot of criticism directed at you. Accounting is much more objective. If the books balance, you know you did your job properly, no matter what other people may think.

Q: What do you like least?

A: Having to make collection calls. Most people were professional, but some had no qualms whatever about lying about when they planned to pay the bills they owed.

Q: What personal qualities do you find most valuable for this type of work?

A: Attention to detail, logic, patience. If you don't have those qualities, you will be miserable in this profession.

Q: What advice do you have for students who might be interested in this career?

A: Take an accounting course. You will know very quickly if this kind of work suits you.

Q: How did you train for your career?

A: I graduated from college with a double major in English and history. Unfortunately, job prospects were not great. I knew I needed more training if I wanted to get a decent-paying job, but I didn't want to commit to more than a year or two of graduate school. So I looked around for programs that could provide training in that time frame. I knew I liked accounting, so I found a program at the Rochester Institute of Technology (RIT) that was perfect for me. It took two years and offered an MBA with a concentration in accounting. So I could kill two birds with one stone: learn accounting *and* get an MBA at the same time.

I had some really good luck while I was at RIT. I had an accounting professor who took an interest in helping his students find good jobs after graduation. This professor used some class time to talk about accounting careers, and he strongly suggested that his students investigate public accounting. His rationale was that, in public accounting, you are exposed to lots of different businesses and you meet lots of different businesspeople, so you can learn a lot in a short time. So I took his advice, interviewed at different public accounting firms, and got a job as an auditor with a major accounting firm called Price Waterhouse after graduation.

Price Waterhouse had a great in-house training program, and it assigned me to teams auditing all different types of businesses. I worked there for three years. During that time, I realized that the clients I enjoyed auditing the most were the small businesses, where I could really get a feel for the entire business rather than only one or two departments. I also was getting a little tired of the traveling that public accounting sometimes required. So I left Price Waterhouse and got a series of accounting jobs in smaller businesses for the rest of my career, and I've been very happy.

Other Jobs in Finance

Actuary
Agent
Bank compliance officer
Bank examiner
Bank manager
Benefits manager
Brokerage clerk
Budget analyst
Business manager
Commodities broker
Cost estimator
Credit analyst
Credit counselor
Development director
Economist
Equity trader
Escrow officer
Estate planner
Financial examiner
Financial manager
Financial reporter/writer
Financial services sales agent

Forecast analyst
Fraud examiner
Gaming cage/casino worker
Insurance appraiser
Insurance underwriter
Investment banking analyst
Market research analyst
Mortgage loan servicing
    manager
Office manager
Payroll clerk
Payroll manager
Real estate broker
Risk management specialist
Securities and commodities sales
    agent
Tax associate
Tax collector
Tax examiner
Tax manager
Tax preparer
Valuation analyst

Editor's Note: The online *Occupational Outlook Handbook* of the US Department of Labor's Bureau of Labor Statistics is an excellent source of information on jobs in hundreds of career fields, including many of those listed here. The *Occupational Outlook Handbook* may be accessed online at www.bls.gov/ooh.

Index

Note: Boldface page numbers indicate illustrations.

accountant(s), 7, 9
  advancement opportunities,
    14–15
  certification/licensing, 10, 12–13
  earnings, 10, 14
  education, 10, 12
  employers of, 14
  future outlook for, 10, 15
  information sources, 15–16
  interview with, 71–73
  number of jobs for, 10
  roles of, 10–12
  skills/personality traits, 10, 13
  volunteer work/internships, 13
  working conditions for, 10, 14
accounts clerk(s), 17
  advancement opportunities, 21
  certification/licensing, 17, 19
  earnings, 17, 20–21
  education, 17, 19
  employers of, 20
  future job outlook for, 17, 21
  information resources, 21–22
  number of jobs for, 17
  roles of, 17–19
  skills/personal qualities, 17,
    19–20
  volunteer work/internships, 19
  working conditions for, 17, 20
American Accounting Association
  (AAA), 15
American Bankers Association

(ABA), 26, 28–29, 60
American Institute of Certified
  Planners (AICP), 41, 44
American Institute of Certified
  Public Accountants (AICPA), 15
American Institute of Professional
  Bookkeepers, 19
American Institute of Professional
  Bookkeepers (AIPB), 21
American Payroll Association, 22
American Planning Association
  (APA), 44
Association for Financial
  Professionals (AFP), 32, 35, 52
auditing clerks, 18
auditors, 12

BAI, 29
bank teller(s), 24
  certification/licensing, 26
  earnings, 22, 27
  education, 22, 26
  employers of, 27
  future job outlook for, 22, 28
  information resources, 28–29
  number of jobs for, 22
  roles of, 23–25
  skills/personal qualities, 22,
    26–27
  volunteer work/internships, 26
  working conditions for, 22, 27
bookkeeping clerks, 18
Bureau of Labor Statistics (BLS),
  74
  on accounting jobs, 15

Picture Credits

Maury Aaseng: 8

Thinkstock Images: 24, 39, 64

About the Author

Joanne Mattern has written many nonfiction books for young people. She enjoys making real-life events and issues come to life for her readers. Mattern comes from a banking family and has always been interested in financial issues. She lives in New York State with her husband, four children, and several pets.